GHP

George's **G** Book

WRITTEN BY **J. L. MAZZEO**

ILLUSTRATED BY **HELEN ROSS REVUTSKY**

dingles&company New Jersey

First Printing

Published By dingles&company
P.O. Box 508
Sea Girt, New Jersey 08750

LIBRARY OF CONGRESS CATALOG CARD NUMBER
2005907194

ISBN
ISBN-13: 978 1-59646-452-0
ISBN-10: 1-59646-452-6

Printed in the United States of America

My Letter Library series is based on the original concept of Judy Mazzeo Zocchi.

ART DIRECTION
Barbie Lambert & Rizco Design
DESIGN
Rizco Design
EDITED BY
Andrea Curley
PROJECT MANAGER
Lisa Aldorasi
EDUCATIONAL CONSULTANT
Maura Ruane McKenna
PRE-PRESS BY
Pixel Graphics

EXPLORE THE LETTERS OF THE ALPHABET WITH MY LETTER LIBRARY*

Aimee's **A** Book
Bebe's **B** Book
Cassie's **C** Book
Delia's **D** Book
Emma's **E** Book
Faye's **F** Book
George's **G** Book
Henry's **H** Book
Izzy's **I** Book
Jade's **J** Book
Kelsey's **K** Book
Logan's **L** Book
Mia's **M** Book
Nate's **N** Book
Owen's **O** Book
Peter's **P** Book
Quinn's **Q** Book
Rosie's **R** Book
Sofie's **S** Book
Tad's **T** Book
Uri's **U** Book
Vera's **V** Book
Will's **W** Book
Xavia's **X** Book
Yola's **Y** Book
Zach's **Z** Book

* All titles also available in bilingual English/Spanish versions.

WEBSITE
www.dingles.com
E-MAIL
info@dingles.com

My **Letter** Library

Gg

My Letter Library leads young children through the alphabet one letter at a time. By focusing on an individual letter in each book, the series allows youngsters to identify and absorb the concept of each letter thoroughly before being introduced to the next. In addition, it invites them to look around and discover where objects beginning with the specific letter appear in their own world.

Gg

A a B b C c D d E e F f **G g**

H h I i J j K k L l M m N n

O o P p Q q R r S s T t U u

V v W w X x Y y Z z

G is for **G**eorge.

George is a **g**entle **g**iraffe.

In George's grassland
you will find
some **g**ooseberries,

Gg

a green **g**rasshopper

looking for lunch,

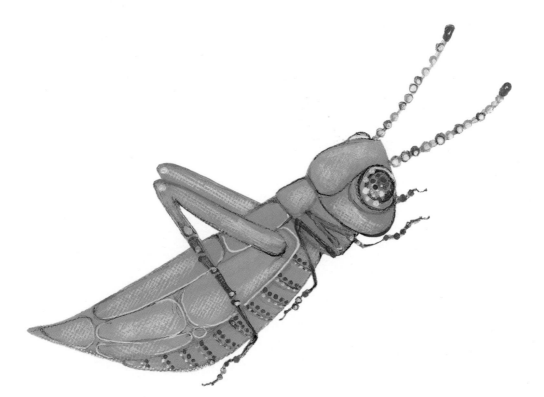

Gg

and a groovy guitar
for making music.

Gg

While spending time
with George you might
see a giggling **g**opher,

G g

some **g**rapes

for making jelly,

Gg

or George's little sister **G**ail.

G g

When visiting George
you might spot
some **g**arlic for cooking,

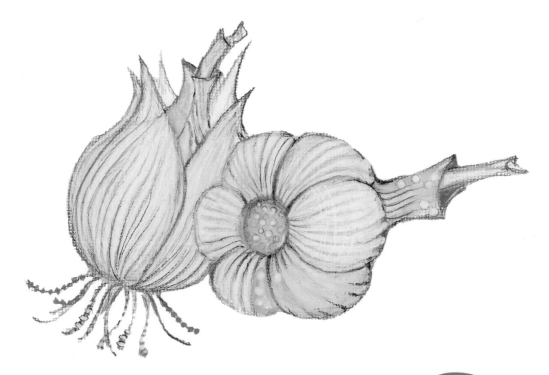

Gg

a **g**lowworm
that has lost his way,

Gg

or a **g**oldfinch flying home.

Gg

Things that begin with the letter **G** are all around.

GOOSEBERRIES

GRASSHOPPER

GUITAR

GOPHER

GRAPES

GAIL

GARLIC

GLOWWORM

GOLDFINCH

Where in
George's grassland
can they be found?

Have a **"G"** Day!

Read "G" stories all day long.
Read books about giraffes, guitars, and other **G** words. Then have the child pick out all of the words and pictures starting with the letter **G**.

Make a "G" Craft: Lollipop Ghost
Have the child draw a face in the middle of a white tissue using a black marker. Place the tissue over a lollipop so that the face is over the candy.

Wrap a rubber band where the lollipop stick and candy meet.

Your child can eat the Lollipop Ghost or make more and hand them out to friends as a spooky treat!

Make a "G" Snack: Groovy Granola
- Have your child place 6 cups of dry, old-fashioned oatmeal in a 9-x-13-inch pan. Toast the oatmeal for 10 minutes at 350 degrees F.
- Next, have him or her combine 1 cup each of sunflower seeds, wheat germ, raisins, nuts, sesame seeds, and coconut in a bowl. (Make sure no one is allergic to anything.)
- In another bowl, help the child combine 1/2 cup of oil, 1 cup of honey, 1/2 cup of sugar, and 2 teaspoons of vanilla. Have him or her stir this into the dry mixture.
- Next, have him or her spread this mixture over the toasted oatmeal and gently mix the two together.
- Return the pan to the oven and bake the mixture at 350 degrees F for 20 to 30 minutes.
- Let the Groovy Granola cool, and enjoy!

For additional **"G"** Day ideas and a reading list, go to www.dingles.com.

About **Letters**

Use the My Letter Library series to teach a child to identify letters and recognize the sounds they make by hearing them used and repeated in each story.

Ask:
- What letter is this book about?
- Can you name all of the **G** pictures on each page?
- Which **G** picture is your favorite? Why?
- Can you find all of the words in this book that begin with the letter **G**?

ENVIRONMENT
Discuss objects that begin with the letter **G** in the child's immediate surroundings and environment.

Use these questions to further the conversation:
- Did you ever see a real giraffe? If so, where?
- Have you ever seen a real guitar? Do you like the sound it makes?
- Have you ever strummed a guitar?
- Do you like to eat grapes? Do you like the green or red ones?

OBSERVATIONS
The My Letter Library series can be used to enhance the child's imagination. Encourage the child to look around and tell you what he or she sees.

Ask:
- Have you ever tasted something that had garlic in it? Did you like how it tasted?
- Pretend you are a giraffe in the grassland. What would you do?
- Do you have a favorite food that begins with the letter **G**? What is it?
- Do you like to giggle? What are some things that make you giggle?

TRY SOMETHING NEW...
The next time it is garbage day in your neighborhood, ask a parent if you can help with the trash. Perhaps you can empty all of the wastebaskets in the house or help your parents put the cans out for collection!

J. L. MAZZEO grew up in Middletown, New Jersey, as part of a close-knit Italian American family. She currently resides in Monmouth County, New Jersey, and still remains close to family members in heart and home.

HELEN ROSS REVUTSKY was born in St. Petersburg, Russia, where she received a degree in stage artistry/ design. She worked as the directing artist in Kiev's famous Governmental Puppet Theatre. Her first book, *I Can Read the Alphabet,* was published in Moscow in 1998. Helen now lives in London, where she has illustrated several children's books.